Sunday Afternoon

a collection of poems about love

SNIGDHA

ISBN 979-8-89322-263-0

poems for you and me

and everyone

who has loved

My dear readers this book is a piece of my heart among many other broken ones to tell you stories about my good and bad days invested in love. This world has always silenced the sensitive ones, pushed in the corner. So, I took a pen and wrote everything I felt. The immense love and pain, anger, resentment and sadness I penned down everything. So now you know you're not alone, I have been there too.

Contents

Chapter 1

prelude to the love story …

untitled 1

when i touched love
for the very first time
it melted down
on my fingers, dancing
around my lips making
me smile little more often
like a warm sunny afternoon
i let myself get soaked
into the feeling

November afternoon

as the mid-afternoon sun
casts shadows on my skin
i recall your face from that day
on an unknown platform
you and me
when you stood so taller than me
november winds pulling us closer
you extend those wide arms
and i stayed hoping it stays forever
caged in this moment forever
you and me
that first picture of us together
shining in the sunlight
under the bougainvillea
blooming pink blossoms
under the open sky
under the sunshine
you and me

Serotonin

a song in my head
it is a fine morning raining
all pouring out love
and i think of you
smiling all along the way
but i am all alone
on my way to the
route, i travel everyday
i leave you behind at home
but i take every piece of you
with me anywhere i go
i have my mind on you
and now i know
it does not really rhyme
but i am writing about you
i do not care who is watching
i will smile all day
you are my serotonin

my love gardener

while the city fell asleep
i was still thinking of you
of your pristine smile and
your uniform perfectly shaped lips
how beautifully you collect
my broken pieces,
how easily your hands unweave
the strings of my heart
transforming a conundrum into
an artistic poetry
oh how naturally the dormant saplings
grew on his bare hands!
just a cordial touch of his soul,
and my love garden
kept blooming...

supernova

my world collides with his;
and like supernova
everything is blazed
yet we were dancing
in the flames

indie music and love freak

i feel so drunk on love
reimagining your hands
on my shoulders
listening indie music in the bar let's leave you say
and i say can't we stay
stuck in this moment frozen
like we've nowhere to hurry
late night you took my hand
and we ran and I screamed
laughing my lungs out
blaring streetlights and honking cars

no heartbreak could break us apart
we stuffed pastries and I licked some
off your mouth and we fell
all over each other again

love me enough

my heart skipped a beat
when i felt your eyes
so closer to mine
like i looked straight
into the vivid cosmos
i fell for everything
in this universe
one where you exist

fire and water

your scars and all of your fears

oh, i have loved you

like the moon and the craters

your imperfections and

your all curves and edges

i have fell for thy heart

that loves too vague

breaks too soft

and you wonder why

i am a hopeless lover

and you dear amour

are a flawless creation

biblical fool

you my sly slithering orphidian
lurking me out the garden of sanity
pursuing me with your delusional charms
making my wild desires true
insisting me to take a leap
to take a bite
of the forbidden love
taste the sinful love
and i a biblical fool
even knowing the consequences
danced to the rhythm of your undertones
and i crossed the line
there was no returning ever

forever and now

take me to a rollercoaster ride

on the backseat of your bike

i feel the wind gushing through my hair

i hold onto tight

singing out loud

our favorite song

melodies intertwined we laugh out loud

when i say goodbye

breaking into tears

he says i am here to stay

tonight, and for the

rest of my life

unfurl

strip down the heavy thoughts
unravel my naked soul
come closer to fire
step into my universe
i have been waiting
for someone to love me
like i loved him

i stayed

barefoot tiptoe you walked in
and became my favorite muse
ignorant i keep wishing for
that you leave and
let it be
but now i see,
you carved your shape
into my vacant space
and the light shines bright,
so bright even my grey space
looks happier now
you finally walked in
and now i'm never leaving

my helios

i dreamt of the fireball,

burning so beautifully in the golden light

when i turned around

i see it in your eyes

a light so bright

blurring my sanity

and i crossed the lines

ran for home searching for the sun

oh so beautifully you

burn down my walls

and i stand feeling so protected

surrounded by your flames

so happily burning into you

drown into you

i was so hard like glass
before i met you, too brittle
i could break easily
covered by my shells
surrounded by walls
i kept building, higher and stronger
each time i break, i bounced back again
faster and stronger
but your calming voice rings in my depth
and it all crumbles down
like a castle of glass
you shatter my world
i've never felt so exposed
your warm touch, i'm naked
and my shell breaks
i'm all soft again
a hopeless romantic
it makes me scared again
i'm too happy
you wrap me around

in depth of your ocean
warm waters singing to me
and i sleep like a baby
i've never felt so safe
you make love look so easy

i've found home

i've cried endless tears
poured out my grief, all to him
and he always cares
filling my cups
with abundant love and embrace
i am thankful, for i am
not existential without you
the happy world we made
handpicking every small
moments of tender and grace
and all the little things he did
held my hand while he
falls asleep and i watched
myself falling in love
all i can do now
is smile and sleep
next to him

apricity

love is the warmth
of the winter sun in november
in the arms of the lover
i reach out to your love
my world is surrounded
by your warm embrace
can you keep me forever?
hope you do,
and we stay
holding it together

love me and how

the way you look at me
while i unfurl my petals
and let them fall, one by one
i can feel your gaze
at me, on my artistry
take me in both of your hands
and drink me in slowly, sip by sip
every drop leaves you spellbound
we fall like a newborn love
pristine and docile
you make no haste
to finish us up in a hurry
reminding me of dried roses
pressed and preserved
between pages of my old notes
my precious finds for the hard times

you keep pouring me
with love and dignity
satin sequin and jewels
would never suffice
the fire and grace of your lips

sugar candy

it's you all over me
like lipstick-stained love letter
scarlet red like blood
burning in my memory
your words swirl around dancing
in my darkest desires
keep me close, but
keep me waiting
i loved the pain, i can love
some more all in your name
and everything falls
right back into place
i have been running my whole life,
only but landing into
this perfect daydream

loving you feels like
sugar candy in my mouth
sweet sour all flavors
bursting butterflies in my belly
and i am falling every night
it is your name and number
i am calling every night

fresh summer

just touch my hand
and let our worlds collide
burning into flames
melting away into each other
my pride my anger shattering
all my handpicked bricks
down to my feet breaking down
onto one another
show me how
to be loved again

golden

just when i thought of you
the sky turned golden
my universe pulling me
onto yours, and i forget
this distance could
not part us

pillow talk

when the morning light
peeking the blinds, hits my face
make sure you keep me close
wrap me up in your arms
like i am the warmest,
safest place
always finding solace
in his fervor whispers

hold me again

there is no safer place
than in your warm embrace
it's like coming back home
after a tiresome day
like a long-lost child
coming back to her mother
i can feel my soul floating away
in a place safer than heaven
where all my sorrows fade away
it does not matter how many
battles i have lost,
with you beside me, i always win
when you wrap me around
my whole universe swirls around
you and your touch
make me see the magic unfold
in your arms

familiar face

here i am again

in your arms feeling like home

and each time our eyes meet

it is like i never left this place

i was always here

with this familiar face

that i call my home

written in stars

i used to chase
this stupid little temporary
curve on their lips
and now we are spinning
the world around us
not hanging by the fragile thread
not anymore
but swinging along
the strong winds in my direction
you are my lifeboat honey
and i saved myself
by being present
right where i was supposed to be

it was all written before
before it all happened
before you and me

February

i remember
that late February
it was the month of love
 our first meeting
when you were on my couch
with the hall room crowded
with so many people
who never cared much
but swallowed me up
in their gaze, finding my flaws
but there you sat
smiling like a baby
and immediately i felt
the butterflies gushing
in my belly to my face
and i can see you blushing

i remember

that warm embrace of your hands

holding me stronger

saying i am staying

and i remember

the last February

when i dressed in red

and called you mine

dear diary

he saw my broken parts
covered with bits and dusts
all over me
insecurities latching onto me
memoirs of many battles lost
yet he called me baby
and something tells me
i was in the right place
at the right time
and my pretty flawed heart
fell a little too hard for you

endless gaze

i am a sucker for words
and yours got stuck
deep in my heart tattooed
in gold letters, breaking me open
with every attempt you climb higher
everest high walls look smaller
closing on me, your soft hands
understand i am an ocean
dive deep, i demand you
to take a leap
those naïve words of mine
sometimes they made no sense
till i found the rhyme in your verse
i am a sucker for love
and the innocence in you
is demanding me to risk it,
to take a leap

vulnerable

i wish if i could
show you my scars
beneath my bare skin,
but would you mind
if my mind grows faster,
than my imagination
if my weeds bloom wildly over your bed
would you mind watering them nice
or would you cut me off
but when i am with you
i could not stop my heart
from feeling your warm smile
on my eyes, kiss upon
my bare cheeks
i am not afraid
to be vulnerable
not when i am with you
i am vulnerable
and somehow you see it

you're my muse

his hands of an angel,
those lips of a sinner
and a belly caged with demons
holds a very fragile muscle within
not merely made of blood & bones
but from earthly air & water
from the flames
burning him down
not just a being to exist
he is my forever muse,
a knot in my heart

daydreams to lilies

when they were painting the roads red
i was falling in love
and it felt a little bit of selfish
to be happy in such time
but lord knows i've been trying
but when the city was crying
i was smiling alone in the nights
daydreaming about the lips
i've never touched, but
i saw him wanting mine

what was long dead is buried now
and here you amaze me
with just one touch
is it me or the love lately,
growing red lilies all over me

when you're alone

make me your sweetest memory
keep me safely hidden
in your distant dreams
always living in your
headspace for free
holding you close
when they all leave

high on love

those beautiful ebony eyes

were addictive enough

to get me drunk

on all those lonely rainy nights

wildfire

your love is contagious
spreading through my veins
faster than any addiction
like wildfire in the forest
making me truly believe
in what they all call love

pulling me stronger

raindrops on my bare cheeks
remind me of when we first kissed
sunshine blinding my eyes
takes me back to the night
when you smiled and i fell hard
but the moon tells me each night
that you're not here anymore
although we were never meant to be
but this universe keeps pulling me
back to you each time

after a long time

walking down the lane
with the setting sun, all alone
my emotions bubbling up ready to burst
more than the bottled soda we shared
i am ahead on my way
lied to all my friends
just to see you once again
your words keep playing replaying
your every i like you, all the way
my breathe becomes heavy,
my blood rushing, it feels
like the first time
i feel my heart pacing
thinking of your pretty face
and there you stand,
at the end of street

there you go again
with that gleaming smile
i want to hug you and
cry the sorrows out,
but a strange lump
grows in my throat
and i just smile at you
all i could say was 'hi'

the sun is up

i have been seeing open wide
roads at every dead-end corner
dreaming of a place echoing
with voices calling my name
this time i did not want to run
but walk straight back to home
to find you on my bed
and the sun is coming up
so are my little hopes
i am gazing into the future
with your arms around me
and this road that i took
will always lead me to you

Chapter 2
the aftermath …

untitled 2

i hope you left me
with a better reason
so i could love again
so i would love myself again
but you only walked
all over me and
brought me shame
and just shame

neither you nor me

oh, my honey
i still miss you
your warm hands and cold heart
filled with love and agony
all for me, nothing for us
that sun glazed tall figure
always protective but held captive
i wonder where your thoughts wander now
that i am no more in your hold now
those stupid selfless giggles
and that homely touch in your arms
it bleeds through my eyes
when i embrace those scars
the empty space of darkness
holding me still captive
did it all began when i stopped
seeing my god
or was it when i opened
my eyes to see who was the god,
neither you nor me

i went to a war and left the battlefield
empty handed, undone i still win
no not you but myself
but oh, my honey
i still miss you
yes, i do

let it go

i could not forgive
but i can let that pass
you do not deserve my pain
or my reason to move beyond
i could not care less but
freedom tastes much better
without you

sad poetry

i am your vengeful story,
you are my sad poetry
the end and the beginning,
never ending loop of love
born and killed and
reborn and murdered
like an unfinished verse
you keep consuming
my mind and my space

are we happy

i am not writing to please your heart
but to justify my wild art
so stop clouding my head
what was that infectious smile;
weren't we happy, truly happy?
turn it all around, did we?
was it so easy to break us?
naïve, my own words feel a shame
back and forth stop tossing my heart
happiness was so fragile

sleep well

i guess nobody
tried so hard to stay
like i did, nobody
was a fool like me
i wonder sometimes
where are you now?
how has life been?
has anyone stayed along?
or have you pushed everyone out
did you find the one?
or are you thriving solitary
are you happier now?
is it keeping you safe,
your distance and boundary?
or do you suffer the same?

i wonder sometimes
if only we were sane,
would you be mine?
or would you run faster?
i guess it is okay now
you are in the shadows
i no longer search
for the shapes in the dark

head and heart

i hate this
you still make me think
wrapping my mind
around your finger
like you still got
hold of my thoughts
sorry i forgot about
the hurt but only
immense sadness
fills the perimeter
of my heart, staining
my every happy memory
into a bloodshed war
with my head and heart
i hoped you cease
to exist someday
but seeing you well

somehow feels

not so sad anymore

guess i moved on

saudade

for years i have been scratching
in the dirt hoping
to find something
valuable something so precious
that i held onto for so long
i lost it's meaning
thinning lines between
right and wrong
we kept switching
from being something into nothing
was it really that i adored you?
or was it just my need
to escape from my myself

running away never
really worked out
you were my home
for the longest time
a home that you
always abandoned

just after love

don’t love me if
all you really want to do
is hate my choices
all my right reasons overlooked
turning me into guilty
every happy memory
tainted by your choices
all my thoughts overshadowed
love could have been easier
only if we were to cooperate
but honey we are always separate
chapters of love and hatred

drain it out of me

i could write you
a sad poetry today
wash it all out of me
direct it all to you
but then again deep down
i know it would be vain
it wouldn't bother your conscience
so i stop, my hands refuse
to bleed for you anymore

contamination

each time i see you,
i feel a lump in my throat
a silent teardrop sneaks out
through my cheeks it escapes
i try hard not to let you know
my eyes cannot stop searching
weren't we over back yesterday
but my heart still keeps hoping
for a better tomorrow
it always hurts
to let you go but
it kills me more
to make you stay

choke out

my scream, does it still echo?
beneath your skin, crawling
in your subconscious mind
do you weep when you sleep?
or do you still dream
of the noose getting tighter
does it get easier to kill now?
knowing you've killed before
does it strike you now?
my eyes, that you have
replaced with many before
does it still burn your bones?

gulping in your pathological lies
does it still bleed?
the cut that you designed
on your own skin

slaughterhouse

every touch every love and concern
everything you ever did was a falsie
made me fall, made it look neat
like a scene from a movie
perfectly planned crime scene
each time you smile,
i know you cheat
work it all out, said to myself
i dig deeper to make you feel complete
gasping for air, i strive for light
you shut me out farther to suffer
to make you stay, is a plight
so i stand and watch you
burn us out into ashes

i'll be waiting

please come back home
honey your arms are so strong
but your soul is just so hollow
you leave me strangled in your arms
those lips feel warm like fire
but your heart
is so cold to your bones
and the places in you
i knew changed
but your face remains the same
i forever wait for a home
that no longer belongs to me

morning routine

does my face ever haunt you?
leaving a long limping sensation
in your body and you cannot move
does my smile keep lingering
in your every thought
every small action reminding
of me but then it hits you
harder than your morning coffee
when you think of all the lies
that killed us,
well, your face still does that

i wished upon a broken star

i wish you stayed

keeping me warm

from the cold

inside my heart

verbena

these recurring dreams
you holding me in your arms
in that old two-bedroom apartment
where i met the broken boy
who was still fighting his monsters
where i cried to those yellow curtains
hugging your clothes cause
you won't come home to me
those purple flowers
wilted in your balcony
i was not supposed to love
nor was i supposed to stay
but i had a thing for broken ones

but why do i still dream about it
do you still miss me
maybe in some other life
maybe in some other dimension
but everywhere i fall apart
and every time you will leave

cause i was made to bleed

and you were never made for

being the love of my life

our favorite movie scene

sometimes i still replay
that old movie scene
again and again in my head
where you held me so close
and kissed me for the last time
you were my favorite poison
and i was your secret love
i know you loved me on some days
but you hide it so perfectly
even from yourself
but now even the thought of you
makes me curl up in my bed

i saw you standing right there
right in front of me
i wanted to turn around
but i walked past you
past you and through your dirt

www.ingramcontent.com/pod-product-compliance
Lightning Source LLC
La Vergne TN
LVHW041236150826
845673LV00008B/2401

* 9 7 9 8 8 9 3 2 2 2 6 3 0 *